Birmingham, 1963

Carole Boston Weatherford

WORDSONG
Honesdale, Pennsylvania

PHOTO CREDITS:
Alabama Department of Archives and History, Montgomery, Alabama: 23
Birmingham Civil Rights Institute: 25, 27
The Birmingham News: 5, 21, 31, 33, 35, 37 (Copyright *The Birmingham News*, 2006. All rights reserved. Reprinted by permission.)
Birmingham Public Library Archives, Catalog #854: 19
Library of Congress: 7, 9, 11, 15, 29
U.S. National Archives & Records Administration: 13
Carole Boston Weatherford: 17

Library of Congress Cataloging-in-Publication Data
Weatherford, Carole Boston.
Birmingham, 1963 / Carole Boston Weatherford.—1st ed.
   p. cm.
   ISBN 978-1-59078-440-2 (hardcover : alk. paper)
1. Bombings—Alabama—Birmingham—Poetry.
2. Sixteenth Street Baptist Church (Birmingham, Ala.)—Poetry.
3. African Americans—Crimes against—
Alabama—Birmingham—Poetry.
4. Hate crimes—Alabama—Birmingham—Poetry.
I. Title.
PS3623.E375B57 2007
811'.6—dc22   2006038105

WORDSONG
An Imprint of Boyds Mills Press, Inc.
815 Church Street
Honesdale, Pennsylvania 18431

To all who made the ultimate sacrifice for freedom.
The struggle continues. —C.B.W.

The year I turned ten
I missed school to march with other children
For a seat at whites-only lunch counters.

Like a junior choir, we chanted "We Shall Overcome."
Then, police loosed snarling dogs and fire hoses on us,
And buses carted us, nine hundred strong, to jail.

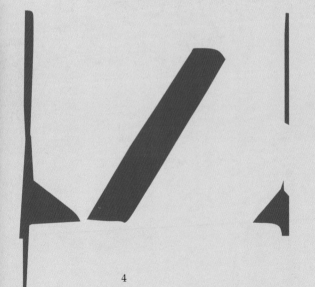

The year I turned ten,
Mama, Daddy, and I stood at Lincoln's feet
While King's dream woke the nation from a long night of wrongs.

Some evenings, I dozed on Mama's shoulder
During mass meetings at church.
The grownups were making big plans.

The day I turned ten
I rehearsed my Youth Day solo in the full-length mirror.
This little light of mine, I'm gonna let it shine.

My little brother sopped red-eye gravy with biscuits
And yanked my pigtails like always,
Poking out his tongue when I tattled.

But Mama allowed me my first sip of coffee
And Daddy twirled me around the kitchen
In my patent-leather cha-cha heels.

Then, our whole family piled into the car
That Daddy had washed and waxed the day before.
We listened to gospel radio as we rode downtown.

The day I turned ten

Our church was quiet. No meetings, no marches.

Mama left me in Sunday school

With a soft kiss and coins for the offering plate.

The teacher read a psalm, told a Bible story,
And led a favorite hymn—
"Jesus Loves the Little Children."

I could hardly wait for church service to begin—
To stand in the pulpit and sing from my heart.
I wiped my clammy palms and took a deep breath.

As I waited, four big girls giggled on their way
To the restroom. I would have tagged along
If I thought they'd include me.

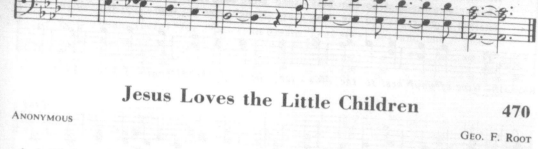

Jesus Loves the Little Children

ANONYMOUS

GEO. F. ROOT

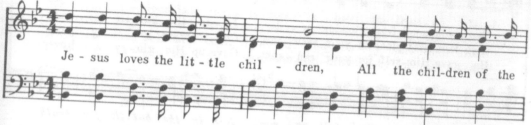

Je - sus loves the lit - tle chil - dren, All the chil-dren of the

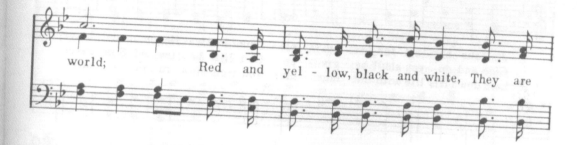

world; Red and yel - low, black and white, They are

pre-cious in His sight; Je - sus loves the lit - tle chil-dren of the world.

The day I turned ten
Someone tucked a bundle of dynamite
Under the church steps, then lit the fuse of hate.

Seconds later, a blast rocked the church.
Smoke clogged my throat, stung my eyes
As I crawled past crumbled plaster, broken glass,
Shredded Bibles and wrecked chairs—
Yelling *Mama! Daddy!*—scared church folk
Ran every-which-way to get out.

That bomb left twenty-one hurt and those four girls—
Cynthia, Denise, Carole, and Addie Mae—dead.
This is my sister, a boy cried. *My God!*

10:22 a.m. The clock stopped, and Jesus' face
Was blown out of the only stained-glass window
Left standing—the one where He stands at the door.
The Lord is my shepherd, said the pastor on a megaphone.

Willing Workers

The day I turned ten,
I saw blood spilled on holy ground
And my daddy cry for the very first time.
What had those girls done to deserve this?

At supper, no one had much appetite.
Afterwards, Mama washed and I dried dishes
While she hummed "Nobody Knows the Trouble I Seen."

By evening, stonings, shootings, and fires broke out.
Keep your children inside, the police warned.
I wondered if I could ever play outside again.

I prayed myself to sleep that night.
Please protect my family, Lord.
God, give four angels wings.

The day I turned ten,

There was no birthday cake with candles;

Just cinders, ash, and a wish I were still nine.

ADDIE MAE COLLINS,

Who sold her mama's handmade aprons

And potholders door-to-door after school.

Who drew portraits, pitched underhand,

Liked hopscotch and bright colors,

And wore her short hair pressed and curled.

The seventh of eight children

Who was the peacemaker

When her brothers and sisters argued.

Addie Mae, who sang in the choir

And starched a white dress for church.

IN MEMORIAM

CYNTHIA WESLEY,

Whose father patrolled their neighborhood,

Nicknamed "Dynamite Hill"

For a string of unsolved bombings.

A mere wisp of a girl in size 2 dresses

That her mother lovingly sewed.

Who sang soul music and sipped sodas

With friends in the backyard.

The carefree girl who traded a class ring

And was like peas in a pod with her buds.

Cynthia, who was always laughing.

IN MEMORIAM

DENISE MCNAIR,
Who liked dolls and put a mudpie
In a mailbox for a childhood crush.
The Brownie, who held tea parties
And staged a yearly fundraiser
In her carport—a neighborhood revue
To fight muscular dystrophy.
Niecie, who always smiled for cameras
And would have been a real go-getter.

IN MEMORIAM

CAROLE ROBERTSON,

Who loved books, earned straight A's,

And took dance lessons every Saturday.

Who joined the Girl Scouts and science club

And played clarinet in the high school band.

A member of Jack and Jill of America.

Carole, who thought she might want

To teach history someday

Or at least make her mark on it.

IN MEMORIAM

AUTHOR'S NOTE

This poem's narrator is fictional, but the events are real. In the 1960s, Birmingham, Alabama, was one of the most racially divided cities in the United States. While civil rights protesters pressed for equality and integration, the staunchest racists resorted to violence to resist change. Racists had set off so many bombs in Birmingham's black neighborhoods that the city was nicknamed "Bombingham."

Sixteenth Street Baptist Church, the city's largest black church, was conveniently located downtown. Thus, many civil rights meetings and rallies were held there. Marches—to integrate lunch counters and to press for better jobs—often started at the church. After one such protest on April 12, 1963, the Reverend Dr. Martin Luther King, Jr., was jailed.

Local civil rights leaders enlisted children—who, if jailed, would not lose wages like adults—for the next round of protests. On May 2, 1963, one thousand children, ranging from six to eighteen years old, gathered in the park across the street from Sixteenth Street Baptist Church and marched downtown, singing "We Shall Overcome." Within hours, nearly nine hundred children were arrested and taken to jails in vans and school buses. The next day, twenty-five hundred more children stayed home from school to join in the protests. That day, police used K-9 dogs and firefighters sprayed high-pressure fire hoses to stop the children's march. The nation was shocked by this police brutality. But Southern racists were even more determined to fight change.

In August 1963, an estimated two hundred fifty thousand people participated in the March on Washington for Jobs and Freedom. There, the Reverend King delivered his famous "I Have a Dream" speech, an appeal for fairness and racial harmony. But that speech did not change some hearts.

On Sunday, September 15, 1963, just before Sunday school ended and the Youth Day worship service began, racists—determined to halt progress—bombed Sixteenth Street Baptist Church. Twenty-one people were injured and four girls were killed: Denise McNair, eleven years old; Carole Robertson, Addie Mae Collins, and Cynthia Wesley, all fourteen. Reaction to the tragedy ranged from shock and dismay to violence. At the funeral for the girls, the Reverend King called them princesses and angels, and prayed that those blinded by hate would one day see beyond skin color.

In 1965, the Federal Bureau of Investigation (FBI) named four suspects in the bombing, but FBI Director J. Edgar Hoover blocked the evidence and no one was charged with the crime. Finally, in 1977, Robert Edward Chambliss was found guilty of the bombing. In 1988, while dying of cancer, Gary Tucker admitted his part in the crime. The convictions of Thomas Blanton, Jr., and Bobby Frank Cherry followed in 2001 and 2002, respectively. Unbelievably, the case was not closed until thirty-nine years after the bombing took place.

NOTES ON THE PHOTOGRAPHS

PAGE 5: On May 2–3, 1963, students of all ages marched in the streets of downtown Birmingham to challenge segregation. Over nine hundred were arrested in what is known as the Children's March. **PAGE 7:** Approximately 250,000 people gathered on the Mall on August 28, 1963, for the March on Washington for Jobs and Freedom. The Reverend Dr. Martin Luther King, Jr., delivered one of the greatest speeches in American history to what was then the largest crowd ever seen in the nation's capital. **PAGE 9:** The Sixteenth Street Baptist Church hosted mass rallies during the civil rights movement and served as a meeting place for activists. **PAGE 11:** In Birmingham and throughout the South, racial segregation laws required that black and white patrons be separated in places such as schools, restaurants, theaters, and bus depot waiting rooms. **PAGE 13:** African American spirituals, freedom songs, and gospel music inspired and unified civil rights protesters. **PAGE 15:** Built in 1911, the Sixteenth Street Baptist Church was designed by Wallace Rayfield, a prominent black architect. The church stood at the center of Birmingham's African American community. **PAGE 19:** Birmingham was home to one of the most violent chapters of the Ku Klux Klan, a race hate group. **PAGE 21:** The explosion—sparked by nineteen sticks of dynamite planted under the church's steps—destroyed the church's rear wall. **PAGE 23:** The face of Christ was knocked out of the only stained-glass window to survive the explosion. **PAGE 25:** Police surveillance photographs recorded events at the church and in the streets. **PAGE 27:** In the wake of the bombing, violence erupted across Birmingham. **PAGE 29:** On September 15, 1963, the Congress of Racial Equality organized a march in memory of the victims.

FURTHER READING

Levine, Ellen. *Freedom's Children: Young Civil Rights Activists Tell Their Own Stories.*
New York: Putnam, 1993.

McWhorter, Diane. *A Dream of Freedom: The Civil Rights Movement from 1954 to 1968.*
New York: Scholastic, 2004.

Meltzer, Milton. *There Comes a Time: The Struggle for Civil Rights.*
New York: Random House, 2001.

Rochelle, Belinda. *Witnesses to Freedom: Young People Who Fought for Civil Rights.*
New York: Lodestar Books, 1993.

WEB SITES*

Birmingham Civil Rights Institute. *www.bcri.org*

Birmingham Public Library Digital Collections—Sixteenth Street Baptist Church.
www.bplonline.org/resources/Digital_Project/SixteenthStBaptistBomb.asp

*Active at the time of publication

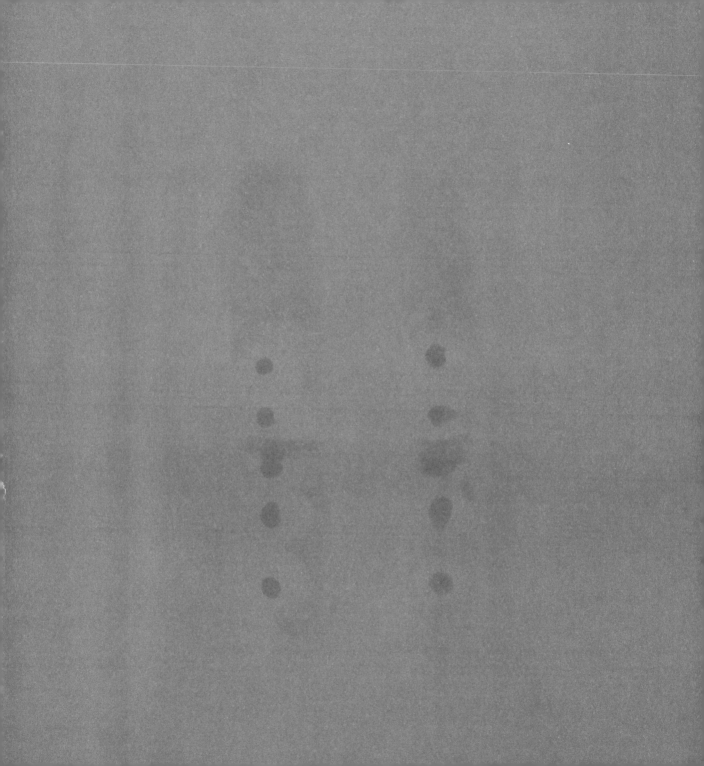